NEW!

LOOK FOR THE CAME[RA]
technique videos made just f[or]

Texting Mitts

LEISURE ARTS, INC. • Little Rock, Arkansas

SIMPLE BEGINNER LACE MITTS

BEGINNER

SHOPPING LIST

Yarn (Super Fine Weight)
[1.76 ounces, 213 yards
(50 grams, 195 meters) per skein]:
☐ One skein

Crochet Hook
☐ Size F (3.75 mm)
   or size needed for gauge

Additional Supplies
☐ Tapestry needle

SIZE INFORMATION

Finished Hand Circumference:
Small - 6¼" (16 cm)
Medium - 6¾" (17 cm)
Large - 7¼" (18.5 cm)

Size Note: We have printed the instructions for the sizes in different colors to make it easier for you to find:
• size Small in Blue
• size Medium in Pink
• size Large in Green
Instructions in Black apply to all sizes.

GAUGE INFORMATION

In Cuff pattern, (sc, ch 2, sc) 5
   times = 2¼" (5.75 cm) and
   11 rnds = 2½" (6.25 cm)
In Body pattern, (dc, ch 2, dc) 4
   times = 2¼" (5.75 cm) and
   5 rows/rnds = 2" (5 cm)

Gauge Swatch:
2½{2¾-3}"w (flattened) x 2¾"h
6.25{7-7.5} cm x 7 cm
Work same as Cuff through Rnd 11:
22{24-26} sc and 11{12-13} ch-2 sps.

INSTRUCTIONS

Mitt (Make 2)

CUFF

Foundation (Right side)**:** Leaving a long end for sewing, ch 67{73-79};
🎥 working in back ridge of chs *(Fig. 2a, page 30)*, sc in second ch from hook, (skip next ch, sc in next ch) across to last ch, skip last ch and being careful **not** to twist piece, slip st in first sc to begin working in rnds: 33{36-39} sc.

Rnd 1: Ch 1, turn; (sc, ch 2, sc) in first sc, skip next 2 sc, ★ (sc, ch 2, sc) in next sc, skip next 2 sc; repeat from ★ around; join with slip st to first sc: 22{24-26} sc and 11{12-13} ch-2 sps.

Rnds 2-11: Turn; slip st in next sc and in next ch-2 sp, ch 1, (sc, ch 2, sc) in same sp and in each ch-2 sp around; join with slip st to first sc.

Do **not** finish off.

BODY

Rnds 1-4: Turn; slip st in next st and in next ch-2 sp, ch 5 (**counts as first dc plus ch 2, now and throughout**), dc in same sp, (dc, ch 2, dc) in next ch-2 sp and in each ch-2 sp around; join with slip st to first dc: 22{24-26} dc and 11{12-13} ch-2 sps.

Do **not** finish off.

THUMB OPENING

Row 1: Ch 3 (**counts as first dc, now and throughout**), turn; (dc, ch 2, dc) in next ch-2 sp and in each ch-2 sp around, dc in same dc as joining, do **not** join: 24{26-28} dc and 11{12-13} ch-2 sps.

Row 2: Ch 3, turn; (dc, ch 2, dc) in next ch-2 sp and in each ch-2 sp across to last 2 dc, skip next dc, dc in last dc.

Row 3: Ch 3, turn; (dc, ch 2, dc) in next ch-2 sp and in each ch-2 sp across to last 2 dc, skip next dc, dc in last dc; slip st in first dc of this row to begin working in rnds.

Next Rnd: Turn; slip st in first 2 dc and in next ch-2 sp, ch 5, dc in same sp, (dc, ch 2, dc) in next ch-2 sp and in each ch-2 sp around; join with slip st to first dc: 22{24-26} dc and 11{12-13} ch-2 sps.

Next 2 Rnds: Turn; slip st in next dc and in next ch-2 sp, ch 5, dc in same sp, (dc, ch 2, dc) in next ch-2 sp and in each ch-2 sp around; join with slip st to first dc.

Last Rnd: Turn; slip st in next dc and in next ch-2 sp, (ch 1, sc in same sp) 4 times, ★ sc in next ch-2 sp, (ch 1, sc in same sp) 3 times; repeat from ★ around; join with slip st to first sc, finish off.

Thread tapestry needle with long end and sew base of beginning ch together.

SMALL V-STITCH WRISTERS

EASY

SHOPPING LIST

Yarn (Super Fine Weight)
[1.75 ounces, 229.6 yards
(50 grams, 210 meters) per skein]:
☐ One skein

Crochet Hook
☐ Size F (3.75 mm)
 or size needed for gauge

Additional Supplies
☐ Tapestry needle

SIZE INFORMATION

Finished Hand Circumference:

Small - 5¾" (14.5 cm)
Medium - 6¼" (16 cm)
Large - 7" (18 cm)

Size Note: We have printed the instructions for the sizes in different colors to make it easier for you to find:
- size Small in Blue
- size Medium in Pink
- size Large in Green

Instructions in Black apply to all sizes.

GAUGE INFORMATION

In pattern, (sc, ch 2, sc) 4 times = 1¾" (4.5 cm) and 8 rnds = 2" (5 cm)

Gauge Swatch:

2¾{3-3½}"w (flattened) x 1½"h
7{7.5-9} cm x 3.75 cm
Work same as Cuff through Rnd 5: 26{28-32} sc and 13{14-16} ch-2 sps.

STITCH GUIDE

FOUNDATION SINGLE CROCHET
(abbreviated Fsc)

Ch 2, insert hook under top 2 loops of second ch from hook, YO and pull up a loop *(Fig. 2b, page 30)*, YO and draw through one loop on hook **(ch made)**, YO and draw through 2 loops on hook **(first Fsc made)**, ★ insert hook under top 2 loops of ch at base of previous Fsc, YO and pull up a loop, YO and draw through one loop on hook **(ch made)**, YO and draw through 2 loops on hook **(Fsc made)**; repeat from ★ for each additional Fsc.

INSTRUCTIONS
Mitt (Make 2)
CUFF

Foundation (Right side)**:** Work 39{42-48} Fsc; being careful **not** to twist piece, join with slip st to first Fsc to begin working in rnds.

Note: Loop a short piece of yarn around any stitch to mark Foundation as **right** side.

Rnd 1: Ch 1, turn; (sc, ch 2, sc) in next Fsc, skip next 2 Fsc, ★ (sc, ch 2, sc) in next Fsc, skip next 2 Fsc; repeat from ★ around; join with slip st to first sc: 26{28-32} sc and 13{14-16} ch-2 sps.

Rnds 2-14: Turn; slip st in next sc and in next ch-2 sp, ch 1, (sc, ch 2, sc) in same sp and in each ch-2 sp around; join with slip st to first sc.

Rnd 15: Turn; slip st in next sc and in next ch-2 sp, ch 1, 4 sc in same sp and in each ch-2 sp around; join with slip st to first sc, finish off.

BODY

Rnd 1: With **right** side facing and working in chs at base of Fsc, join yarn with sc in ch at base of first Fsc *(see Joining With Sc, page 29)*; ch 2, sc in same st, skip next 2 chs, ★ (sc, ch 2, sc) in next ch, skip next 2 chs; repeat from ★ around; join with slip st to first sc: 26{28-32} sc and 13{14-16} ch-2 sps.

Rnds 2-9: Turn; slip st in next sc and in next ch-2 sp, ch 1, (sc, ch 2, sc) in same sp and in each ch-2 sp around; join with slip st to first sc.

www.leisurearts.com

Do **not** finish off.

THUMB OPENING

Row 1: Ch 1, turn; sc in next sc, (sc, ch 2, sc) in next ch-2 sp and in each ch-2 sp around, hdc in next sc; do **not** join: 28{30-34} sts and 13{14-16} ch-2 sps.

Rows 2 and 3: Ch 1, turn; sc in first hdc, (sc, ch 2, sc) in next ch-2 sp and in each ch-2 sp across to last 2 sc, skip next sc, hdc in last sc.

Row 4: Ch 1, turn; sc in first hdc, (sc, ch 2, sc) in next ch-2 sp and in each ch-2 sp across to last 2 sc, skip next sc, hdc in last sc, skip first sc of this row and join with slip st in second sc to begin working in rnds.

Next Rnd: Turn; slip st in next 2 sts and in next ch-2 sp, ch 1, (sc, ch 2, sc) in same sp and in each ch-2 sp around; join with slip st to first sc.

Next 7 Rnds: Turn; slip st in next sc and in next ch-2 sp, ch 1, (sc, ch 2, sc) in same sp and in each ch-2 sp around; join with slip st to first sc.

Last Rnd: Turn; slip st in next sc and in next ch-2 sp, ch 1, 4 sc in same sp and in each ch-2 sp around; join with slip st to first sc, finish off.

DIAMOND BACK MITTS

■■■□ INTERMEDIATE

SHOPPING LIST

Yarn (Super Fine Weight) [1]
[3.5 ounces, 438 yards
(100 grams, 400 meters) per skein]:
☐ One skein

Crochet Hook
☐ Size E (3.5 mm)
   or size needed for gauge

Additional Supplies
☐ Tapestry needle

SIZE INFORMATION

Finished Hand Circumference:

Small - 6$5/8$" (17 cm)
Medium - 7" (18 cm)
Large - 7$3/8$" (18.5 cm)

Size Note: We have printed the instructions for the sizes in different colors to make it easier for you to find:
- size Small in Blue
- size Medium in Pink
- size Large in Green

Instructions in Black apply to all sizes.

GAUGE INFORMATION

24 dc and 12 rnds = 4" (10 cm)
In Cuff pattern, 15 sts = 2" (5 cm)

Gauge Swatch:
   2$5/8${2$3/4$-3}"w (flattened) x 2$1/8$"h
   6.75{7-7.5} cm x 5.5 cm
Work same as Cuff, page 8, through Rnd 10: 40{42-44} sts.

STITCH GUIDE

FOUNDATION SINGLE CROCHET
   (abbreviated Fsc)

Ch 2, insert hook under top 2 loops of second ch from hook, YO and pull up a loop *(Fig. 2b, page 30)*, YO and draw through one loop on hook (**ch made**), YO and draw through 2 loops on hook (**first Fsc made**), ★ insert hook under top 2 loops of ch at base of previous Fsc, YO and pull up a loop, YO and draw through one loop on hook (**ch made**), YO and draw through 2 loops on hook (**Fsc made**); repeat from ★ for each additional Fsc.

TREBLE CROCHET
   (abbreviated tr)

YO twice, insert hook in st or sp indicated, YO and pull up a loop (4 loops on hook), (YO and draw through 2 loops on hook) 3 times.

FRONT HALF DOUBLE CROCHET
   (abbreviated front hdc)

YO, insert hook from **front** to **back** around top of next st *(Fig. 4, page 30)*, YO and pull up a loop, YO and draw through all 3 loops on hook.

BACK HALF DOUBLE CROCHET
   (abbreviated back hdc)

YO, insert hook from **back** to **front** around top of next st *(Fig. 4, page 30)*, YO and pull up a loop, YO and draw through all 3 loops on hook.

FRONT POST TREBLE CROCHET CLUSTER
   (abbreviated FPtr Cluster)

★ YO twice, insert hook from **front** to **back** around post of st indicated *(Fig. 3, page 30)*, YO and pull up a loop, (YO and draw through 2 loops on hook) twice; repeat from ★ once **more**, YO and draw through all 3 loops on hook.

CLUSTER CROSS ST
   (uses next 3 sts)

Skip next 2 sts, work FPtr Cluster around next st, ch 1, working in **front** of FPtr Cluster just made, work FPtr Cluster around first skipped st.

CLUSTER RIGHT CROSS ST
   (uses next 3 sts)

Skip next 2 sts, work FPtr Cluster around next st, ch 1, working **behind** FPtr Cluster just made, tr in first skipped st.

CLUSTER LEFT CROSS ST
   (uses next 3 sts)

Skip next 2 sts, tr in next st, ch 1, working in **front** of tr just made, work FPtr Cluster around first skipped st.

DOUBLE CROCHET 2 TOGETHER
   (abbreviated dc2tog)
   (uses next 2 sts)

★ YO, insert hook in **next** st, YO and pull up a loop, YO and draw through 2 loops on hook; repeat from ★ once **more**, YO and draw through all 3 loops on hook (**counts as one dc**).

7

INSTRUCTIONS
Mitt (Make 2)
CUFF

Foundation (Right side)**:** Leaving a long end for sewing, work 40{42-44} Fsc; being careful **not** to twist piece, join with slip st to first Fsc to begin working in rnds.

Rnd 1: Ch 2, hdc in same st as joining and in each Fsc around; skip beginning ch-2 and join with slip st to first hdc.

Rnds 2-10: Ch 2, front hdc around same st as joining, back hdc around next st, (front hdc around next st, back hdc around next st) around; skip beginning ch-2 and join with slip st to first front hdc.

Do **not** finish off.

BODY

Rnds 1 and 2: Ch 3 (**counts as first dc, now and throughout**), dc in next st and in each st around; join with slip st to first dc.

Rnd 3: Ch 3, dc in next 18{19-20} dc, skip next 2 dc, work FPtr Cluster around next dc, ch 1, working **behind** FPtr Cluster just made, work FPtr Cluster around first skipped dc, dc in last 18{19-20} sts; join with slip st to first dc: 37{39-41} dc, 2 FPtr Clusters, and one ch.

Right-Hand Mitt

Rnd 4: Ch 3, dc in next 16{17-18} dc, work Cluster Right Cross St, ch 1, skip next ch, work Cluster Left Cross St, dc in next 10{11-11} dc, 2 dc in next dc, dc in last 5{5-6} dc; join with slip st to first dc: 36{38-40} sts, 2 FPtr Clusters, and 3 chs.

Rnd 5: Ch 3, dc in next 14{15-16} dc, work Cluster Right Cross St, ch 1, skip next ch, work Cluster Cross St, ch 1, skip next ch, work Cluster Left Cross St, dc in next 8{9-9} dc, ch 8, skip next 2 dc (**thumb opening**), dc in last 5{5-6} dc; join with slip st to first dc: 30{32-34} sts, 4 FPtr Clusters, one ch-8 sp, and 5 chs.

Rnd 6: Ch 3, dc in next 12{13-14} dc, work Cluster Right Cross St, ch 1, skip next ch, work Cluster Right Cross St, dc in next ch-1 sp, work Cluster Left Cross St, ch 1, skip next ch, work Cluster Left Cross St, dc in next 6{7-7} dc, 4 sc in next ch-8 sp, dc in last 5{5-6} dc; join with slip st to first dc: 33{35-37} sts, 4 FPtr Clusters, and 6 chs.

Rnd 7: Ch 3, dc in next 12{13-14} dc, work Cluster Left Cross St, ch 1, skip next ch, work Cluster Left Cross St, dc in next dc, work Cluster Right Cross St, ch 1, skip next ch, work Cluster Right Cross St, dc in next 5{6-6} dc, dc2tog 3 times, dc in last 4{4-5} dc; join with slip st to first dc, do **not** finish off: 30{32-34} sts, 4 FPtr Clusters, and 6 chs.

Left-Hand Mitt

Rnd 4: Ch 3, dc in next 5{5-6} dc, 2 dc in next dc, dc in next 10{11-11} dc, work Cluster Right Cross St, ch 1, skip next ch, work Cluster Left Cross St, dc in last 16{17-18} dc; join with slip st to first dc: 36{38-40} sts, 2 FPtr Clusters, and 3 chs.

Rnd 5: Ch 3, dc in next 5{5-6} dc, ch 8, skip next 2 dc (**thumb opening**), dc in next 8{9-9} dc, work Cluster Right Cross St, ch 1, skip next ch, work Cluster Cross St, ch 1, skip next ch, work Cluster Left Cross St, dc in last 14{15-16} dc; join with slip st to first dc: 30{32-34} sts, 4 FPtr Clusters, one ch-8 sp, and 5 chs.

Rnd 6: Ch 3, dc in next 5{5-6} dc, 4 sc in next ch-8 sp, dc in next 6{7-7} dc, work Cluster Right Cross St, ch 1, skip next ch, work Cluster Right Cross St, dc in next ch-1 sp, work Cluster Left Cross St, ch 1, skip next ch, work Cluster Left Cross St, dc in last 12{13-14} dc; join with slip st to first dc: 33{35-37} sts, 4 FPtr Clusters, and 6 chs.

Rnd 7: Ch 3, dc in next 4{4-5} dc, dc2tog 3 times, dc in next 5{6-6} dc, work Cluster Left Cross St, ch 1, skip next ch, work Cluster Left Cross St, dc in next dc, work Cluster Right Cross St, ch 1, skip next ch, work Cluster Right Cross St, dc in last 12{13-14} dc; join with slip st to first dc, do **not** finish off: 30{32-34} sts, 4 FPtr Clusters, and 6 chs.

Both Mitts
Rnd 8: Ch 3, dc in next 13{14-15} sts and in next ch-1 sp, work Cluster Left Cross St, ch 1, skip next ch, work Cluster Cross St, ch 1, skip next ch, work Cluster Right Cross St, dc in next ch-1 sp and in last 13{14-15} sts; join with slip st to first dc: 31{33-35} sts, 4 FPtr Clusters, and 5 chs.

Rnd 9: Ch 3, dc in next 15{16-17} sts and in next ch-1 sp, work Cluster Left Cross St, ch 1, skip next ch, work Cluster Right Cross St, dc in next ch-1 sp and in last 15{16-17} sts; join with slip st to first dc: 35{37-39} sts, 2 FPtr Clusters, and 3 chs.

Rnd 10: Ch 3, dc in next 17{18-19} sts and in next ch-1 sp, work Cluster Cross St, dc in next ch-1 sp and in last 17{18-19} sts; join with slip st to first dc: 37{39-41} sts, 2 FPtr Clusters, and one ch.

Rnd 11: Ch 3, dc in next st and in each st and each ch-1 sp around; join with slip st to first dc: 40{42-44} dc.

Rnd 12: Ch 3, dc in next dc and in each dc around; join with slip st to first dc, do **not** finish off.

FINGER RIBBING
Rnd 1: Ch 2, hdc in same st as joining and in each dc around; skip beginning ch-2 and join with slip st to first hdc.

Rnds 2 and 3: Ch 2, front hdc around same st as joining, back hdc around next st, (front hdc around next st, back hdc around next st) around; skip beginning ch-2 and join with slip st to first front hdc; at end of Rnd 3, finish off.

Thread tapestry needle with long end and sew base of Fsc together.

SEASHELL MITTS

EASY

SHOPPING LIST

Yarn (Super Fine Weight) **SUPER FINE 1**
[1.75 ounces, 166 yards
(50 grams, 152 meters) per skein]:
☐ One skein

Crochet Hook
☐ Size F (3.75 mm)
    or size needed for gauge

Additional Supplies
☐ Tapestry needle

SIZE INFORMATION
Finished Hand Circumference:
  7" (18 cm)

GAUGE INFORMATION
In Cross St pattern, 5 Cross Sts (10 dc)
  and 6 rnds = 2¼" (5.75 cm)
In Body pattern,
  3 repeats = 4¼" (10.75 cm)
Gauge Swatch:
  3¼"w (flattened) x 3¼"h
  (8.25 cm x 8.25 cm)
Work same as Cuff through Rnd 8:
30 dc (15 Cross Sts).

STITCH GUIDE
🎥 **CROSS ST** (uses next 2 sts)
Skip next st, dc in next st, working **around** dc just made, dc in skipped st.

INSTRUCTIONS
Mitt (Make 2)
CUFF
Foundation (Right side)**:** Leaving a long end for sewing, ch 61;
🎥 **working in back ridge of chs** *(Fig. 2a, page 30)*, sc in second ch from hook, (skip next ch, sc in next ch) across to last ch, skip last ch and being careful **not** to twist piece, slip st in first sc to begin working in rnds: 30 sc.

Rnd 1: Ch 3 **(counts as first dc, now and throughout)**, working **around** dc just made, dc in last sc made on Foundation **(first Cross St made)**, work Cross Sts around; join with slip st to first dc: 30 dc (15 Cross Sts).

Rnds 2-8: Ch 3, working **around** dc just made, dc in last dc made on previous rnd **(first Cross St made)**, work Cross Sts around; join with slip st to first dc.

Do **not** finish off.

BODY
Rnd 1: Ch 1, sc in same st as joining, ch 1, sc in next dc, skip next 2 dc, (2 dc, ch 1, 2 dc) 🎥 **in sp before next dc** *(Fig. 5, page 30)*, skip next 2 dc, ★ sc in next dc, ch 1, sc in next dc, skip next 2 dc, (2 dc, ch 1, 2 dc) in sp **before** next dc, skip next 2 dc; repeat from ★ around; join with slip st to first sc: 30 sts and 10 ch-1 sps.

THUMB GUSSET
Right-Hand Mitt
Rnd 2: Turn; slip st in next 2 dc and in next ch-1 sp, ch 1, (sc, ch 1, sc) in same sp, (2 dc, ch 1, 2 dc) in next ch-1 sp, (sc, ch 1, sc) in next ch-1 sp, dc in next ch-1 sp, (ch 1, dc in same sp) 3 times, ★ (sc, ch 1, sc) in next ch-1 sp, (2 dc, ch 1, 2 dc) in next ch-1 sp; repeat from ★ around; join with slip st to first sc: 30 sts and 12 ch-1 sps.

Rnd 3: Turn; slip st in next 2 dc and in next ch-1 sp, ch 1, (sc, ch 1, sc) in same sp, (2 dc, ch 1, 2 dc) in next ch-1 sp, ★ (sc, ch 1, sc) in next ch-1 sp, (2 dc, ch 1, 2 dc) in next ch-1 sp; repeat from ★ once **more**, sc in next ch-1 sp, (2 dc, ch 1, 2 dc) in next ch-1 sp, sc in next ch-1 sp, (2 dc, ch 1, 2 dc) in next ch-1 sp, (sc, ch 1, sc) in next ch-1 sp, (2 dc, ch 1, 2 dc) in last ch-1 sp; join with slip st to first sc: 34 sts and 10 ch-1 sps.

11

Rnd 4: Turn; slip st in next 2 dc and in next ch-1 sp, ch 1, (sc, ch 1, sc) in same sp, (2 dc, ch 1, 2 dc) in next ch-1 sp, (sc, ch 1, sc) in next ch-1 sp, [skip next 2 dc, (2 dc, ch 1, 2 dc) in next sc, (sc, ch 1, sc) in next ch-1 sp] twice, (2 dc, ch 1, 2 dc) in next ch-1 sp, ★ (sc, ch 1, sc) in next ch-1 sp, (2 dc, ch 1, 2 dc) in next ch-1 sp; repeat from ★ once **more**; join with slip st to first sc: 36 sts and 12 ch-1 sps.

Rnd 5: Turn; slip st in next 2 dc and in next ch-1 sp, ch 1, (sc, ch 1, sc) in same sp, ★ (2 dc, ch 1, 2 dc) in next ch-1 sp, (sc, ch 1, sc) in next ch-1 sp; repeat from ★ 2 times **more**, dc in next ch-1 sp, (ch 1, dc in same sp) 3 times, [(sc, ch 1, sc) in next ch-1 sp, (2 dc, ch 1, 2 dc) in next ch-1 sp] twice; join with slip st to first sc: 36 sts and 14 ch-1 sps.

Rnd 6: Turn; slip st in next 2 dc and in next ch-1 sp, ch 1, (sc, ch 1, sc) in same sp, (2 dc, ch 1, 2 dc) in next ch-1 sp, (sc, ch 1, sc) in next ch-1 sp, (2 dc, ch 1, 2 dc) in next ch-1 sp, sc in next ch-1 sp, (2 dc, ch 1, 2 dc) in next ch-1 sp, sc in next ch-1 sp, (2 dc, ch 1, 2 dc) in next ch-1 sp, ★ (sc, ch 1, sc) in next ch-1 sp, (2 dc, ch 1, 2 dc) in next ch-1 sp; repeat from ★ 2 times **more**; join with slip st to first sc: 40 sts and 12 ch-1 sps.

Rnd 7: Turn; slip st in next 2 dc and in next ch-1 sp, ch 1, (sc, ch 1, sc) in same sp, ★ (2 dc, ch 1, 2 dc) in next ch-1 sp, (sc, ch 1, sc) in next ch-1 sp; repeat from ★ 2 times **more**, [skip next 2 dc, (2 dc, ch 1, 2 dc) in next sc, (sc, ch 1, sc) in next ch-1 sp] twice, (2 dc, ch 1, 2 dc) in next ch-1 sp, (sc, ch 1, sc) in next ch-1 sp, (2 dc, ch 1, 2 dc) in last ch-1 sp; join with slip st to first sc: 42 sts and 14 ch-1 sps.

Rnd 8: Turn; slip st in next 2 dc and in next ch-1 sp, ch 1, (sc, ch 1, sc) in same sp, (2 dc, ch 1, 2 dc) in next ch-1 sp, ★ (sc, ch 1, sc) in next ch-1 sp, (2 dc, ch 1, 2 dc) in next ch-1 sp; repeat from ★ around; join with slip st to first sc.

Gusset Joining Rnd: Turn; slip st in next 2 dc and in next ch-1 sp, ch 1, (sc, ch 1, sc) in same sp, (2 dc, ch 1, 2 dc) in next ch-1 sp, ★ (sc, ch 1, sc) in next ch-1 sp, (2 dc, ch 1, 2 dc) in next ch-1 sp; repeat from ★ once **more**, sc in next ch-1 sp, ch 1, skip next 3 ch-1 sps (**thumb opening**), sc in next ch-1 sp, (2 dc, ch 1, 2 dc) in next ch-1 sp, (sc, ch 1, sc) in next ch-1 sp, (2 dc, ch 1, 2 dc) in last ch-1 sp; join with slip st to first sc: 30 sts and 10 ch-1 sps.

Last 4 Rnds: Turn; slip st in next 2 dc and in next ch-1 sp, ch 1, (sc, ch 1, sc) in same sp, (2 dc, ch 1, 2 dc) in next ch-1 sp, ★ (sc, ch 1, sc) in next ch-1 sp, (2 dc, ch 1, 2 dc) in next ch-1 sp; repeat from ★ around; join with slip st to first sc.

Finish off.

Thread tapestry needle with long end and sew base of beginning ch together.

Left-Hand Mitt

Rnd 2: **Turn**; slip st in next 2 dc and in next ch-1 sp, ch 1, (sc, ch 1, sc) in same sp, ★ (2 dc, ch 1, 2 dc) in next ch-1 sp, (sc, ch 1, sc) in next ch-1 sp; repeat from ★ 2 times **more**, dc in next ch-1 sp, (ch 1, dc in same sp) 3 times, (sc, ch 1, sc) in next ch-1 sp, (2 dc, ch 1, 2 dc) in last ch-1 sp; join with slip st to first sc: 30 sts and 12 ch-1 sps.

Rnd 3: Turn; slip st in next 2 dc and in next ch-1 sp, ch 1, (sc, ch 1, sc) in same sp, (2 dc, ch 1, 2 dc) in next ch-1 sp, sc in next ch-1 sp, (2 dc, ch 1, 2 dc) in next ch-1 sp, sc in next ch-1 sp, (2 dc, ch 1, 2 dc) in next ch-1 sp, ★ (sc, ch 1, sc) in next ch-1 sp, (2 dc, ch 1, 2 dc) in next ch-1 sp; repeat from ★ 2 times **more**; join with slip st to first sc: 34 sts and 10 ch-1 sps.

Rnd 4: Turn; slip st in next 2 dc and in next ch-1 sp, ch 1, (sc, ch 1, sc) in same sp, ★ (2 dc, ch 1, 2 dc) in next ch-1 sp, (sc, ch 1, sc) in next ch-1 sp; repeat from ★ 2 times **more,** [skip next 2 dc, (2 dc, ch 1, 2 dc) in next sc, (sc, ch 1, sc) in next ch-1 sp] twice, (2 dc, ch 1, 2 dc) in last ch-1 sp; join with slip st to first sc: 36 sts and 12 ch-1 sps.

Rnd 5: Turn; slip st in next 2 dc and in next ch-1 sp, ch 1, (sc, ch 1, sc) in same sp, (2 dc, ch 1, 2 dc) in next ch-1 sp, (sc, ch 1, sc) in next ch-1 sp, dc in next ch-1 sp, (ch 1, dc in same sp) 3 times, ★ (sc, ch 1, sc) in next ch-1 sp, (2 dc, ch 1, 2 dc) in next ch-1 sp; repeat from ★ around; join with slip st to first sc: 36 sts and 14 ch-1 sps.

Rnd 6: Turn; slip st in next 2 dc and in next ch-1 sp, ch 1, (sc, ch 1, sc) in same sp, (2 dc, ch 1, 2 dc) in next ch-1 sp, ★ (sc, ch 1, sc) in next ch-1 sp, (2 dc, ch 1, 2 dc) in next ch-1 sp; repeat from ★ 2 times **more**, sc in next ch-1 sp, (2 dc, ch 1, 2 dc) in next ch-1 sp, sc in next ch-1 sp, (2 dc, ch 1, 2 dc) in next ch-1 sp, (sc, ch 1, sc) in next ch-1 sp, (2 dc, ch 1, 2 dc) in last ch-1 sp; join with slip st to first sc: 40 sts and 12 ch-1 sps.

Rnd 7: Turn; slip st in next 2 dc and in next ch-1 sp, ch 1, (sc, ch 1, sc) in same sp, (2 dc, ch 1, 2 dc) in next ch-1 sp, (sc, ch 1, sc) in next ch-1 sp, [skip next 2 dc, (2 dc, ch 1, 2 dc) in next sc, (sc, ch 1, sc) in next ch-1 sp] twice, (2 dc, ch 1, 2 dc) in next ch-1 sp, ★ (sc, ch 1, sc) in next ch-1 sp, (2 dc, ch 1, 2 dc) in next ch-1 sp; repeat from ★ 2 times **more**; join with slip st to first sc: 42 sts and 14 ch-1 sps.

Rnd 8: Turn; slip st in next 2 dc and in next ch-1 sp, ch 1, (sc, ch 1, sc) in same sp, (2 dc, ch 1, 2 dc) in next ch-1 sp, ★ (sc, ch 1, sc) in next ch-1 sp, (2 dc, ch 1, 2 dc) in next ch-1 sp; repeat from ★ around; join with slip st to first sc.

Gusset Joining Rnd: Turn; slip st in next 2 dc and in next ch-1 sp, ch 1, (sc, ch 1, sc) in same sp, (2 dc, ch 1, 2 dc) in next ch-1 sp, sc in next ch-1 sp, ch 1, skip next 3 ch-1 sps **(thumb opening)**, sc in next ch-1 sp, (2 dc, ch 1, 2 dc) in next ch-1 sp, ★ (sc, ch 1, sc) in next ch-1 sp, (2 dc, ch 1, 2 dc) in next ch-1 sp; repeat from ★ around; join with slip st to first sc: 30 sts and 10 ch-1 sps.

Last 4 Rnds: Turn; slip st in next 2 dc and in next ch-1 sp, ch 1, (sc, ch 1, sc) in same sp, (2 dc, ch 1, 2 dc) in next ch-1 sp, ★ (sc, ch 1, sc) in next ch-1 sp, (2 dc, ch 1, 2 dc) in next ch-1 sp; repeat from ★ around; join with slip st to first sc.

Finish off.

Thread tapestry needle with long end and sew base of beginning ch together.

CABLED SHELLS MITTS

EASY +

SHOPPING LIST

Yarn (Super Fine Weight)
[1.76 ounces, 191 yards
(50 grams, 175 meters) per skein]:
☐ One skein

Crochet Hook
☐ Size E (3.5 mm)
or size needed for gauge

Additional Supplies
☐ Tapestry needle

SIZE INFORMATION

Finished Hand Circumference:
7½" (19 cm)

GAUGE INFORMATION

In Finger Ribbing pattern,
  15 sts = 2" (5 cm)
In Body pattern,
  2 repeats (20 sts) = 3" (7.5 cm);
  6 rnds = 1¾" (4.5 cm)

Gauge Swatch:
  3½"w (flattened) x 1⅛"h
  (9 cm x 2.75 cm)
Work same as Finger Ribbing, page 16, through Rnd 4: 50 sts.

STITCH GUIDE

FOUNDATION SINGLE CROCHET
(abbreviated Fsc)

Ch 2, insert hook under top 2 loops of second ch from hook, YO and pull up a loop *(Fig. 2b, page 30)*, YO and draw through one loop on hook (**ch made**), YO and draw through 2 loops on hook (**first Fsc made**), ★ insert hook under top 2 loops of ch at base of previous Fsc, YO and pull up a loop, YO and draw through one loop on hook (**ch made**), YO and draw through 2 loops on hook (**Fsc made**); repeat from ★ for each additional Fsc.

FRONT HALF DOUBLE CROCHET
(abbreviated front hdc)

YO, insert hook from **front** to **back** around top of next st *(Fig. 4, page 30)*, YO and pull up a loop, YO and draw through all 3 loops on hook.

BACK HALF DOUBLE CROCHET
(abbreviated back hdc)

YO, insert hook from **back** to **front** around top of next st *(Fig. 4, page 30)*, YO and pull up a loop, YO and draw through all 3 loops on hook.

FRONT POST DOUBLE CROCHET
(abbreviated FPdc)

YO, insert hook from **front** to **back** around post of st indicated *(Fig. 3, page 30)*, YO and pull up a loop (3 loops on hook), (YO and draw through 2 loops on hook) twice.

DECREASE (uses next 4 dc)

YO, insert hook in next dc, YO and pull up a loop (3 loops on hook), YO and draw through 2 loops on hook, YO, skip next 2 dc, insert hook in next dc, YO and pull up a loop (4 loops on hook), YO and draw through 2 loops on hook, YO and draw through all 3 loops on hook (**counts as one dc**).

15

INSTRUCTIONS
Mitt (Make 2)
FINGER RIBBING

Foundation (Right side)**:** Leaving a long end for sewing, work 50 Fsc; being careful **not** to twist piece, join with slip st to first Fsc to begin working in rnds.

Rnds 1-4: Ch 2, front hdc around same st as joining, back hdc around next st, (front hdc around next st, back hdc around next st) around; skip beginning ch-2 and join with slip st to first front hdc.

Do **not** finish off.

BODY

Rnd 1: Ch 4, 3 dc in same st as joining, skip next 3 sts, dc in next st, ch 1, skip next st, dc in next st, skip next 3 sts, ★ (3 dc, ch 1, 3 dc) in next st, skip next 3 sts, dc in next st, ch 1, skip next st, dc in next st, skip next 3 sts; repeat from ★ around, 2 dc in same st as first dc; join with slip st to third ch of beginning ch-4: 40 sts and 10 ch-1 sps.

Rnd 2: (Slip st, ch 4, 3 dc) in next ch-1 sp, skip next 3 dc, work FPdc around next dc, ch 1, work FPdc around next dc, ★ (3 dc, ch 1, 3 dc) in next ch-1 sp, skip next 3 dc, work FPdc around next dc, ch 1, work FPdc around next dc; repeat from ★ around, 2 dc in same sp as first dc; join with slip st to third ch of beginning ch-4.

Rnd 3: (Slip st, ch 4, dc) in next ch-1 sp, skip next 3 dc, work FPdc around next FPdc, (2 dc, ch 1, 2 dc) in next ch-1 sp, work FPdc around next FPdc, ★ (dc, ch 1, dc) in next ch-1 sp, skip next 3 dc, work FPdc around next FPdc, (2 dc, ch 1, 2 dc) in next ch-1 sp, work FPdc around next FPdc; repeat from ★ around; join with slip st to third ch of beginning ch-4.

Rnd 4: Ch 4, skip next dc, work FPdc around next FPdc, (3 dc, ch 1, 3 dc) in next ch-1 sp, skip next 2 dc, work FPdc around next FPdc, ★ ch 1, skip next 2 dc, work FPdc around next FPdc, (3 dc, ch 1, 3 dc) in next ch-1 sp, skip next 2 dc, work FPdc around next FPdc; repeat from ★ around; join with slip st to third ch of beginning ch-4.

Rnd 5: Ch 4, work FPdc around next FPdc, (3 dc, ch 1, 3 dc) in next ch-1 sp, skip next 3 dc, work FPdc around next FPdc, ★ ch 1, work FPdc around next FPdc, (3 dc, ch 1, 3 dc) in next ch-1 sp, skip next 3 dc, work FPdc around next FPdc; repeat from ★ around; join with slip st to third ch of beginning ch-4.

Rnd 6: Ch 3, (3 dc, ch 1, 3 dc) in next ch-1 sp, work FPdc around next FPdc, (dc, ch 1, dc) in next ch-1 sp, skip next 3 dc, work FPdc around next FPdc, ★ (2 dc, ch 1, 2 dc) in next ch-1 sp, work FPdc around next FPdc, (dc, ch 1, dc) in next ch-1 sp, skip next 3 dc, work FPdc around next FPdc; repeat from ★ around; join with slip st to top of beginning ch-3.

Rnd 7: Ch 3, 2 dc in next dc, 3 dc in next dc, ch 7, skip next ch-1 sp and next dc (**thumb opening**), 3 dc in each of next 2 dc, work FPdc around next FPdc, ch 1, skip next 2 dc, work FPdc around next FPdc, ★ (3 dc, ch 1, 3 dc) in next ch-1 sp, skip next 2 dc, work FPdc around next FPdc, ch 1, skip next 2 dc, work FPdc around next FPdc; repeat from ★ around; join with slip st to top of beginning ch-3.

Rnd 8: Ch 3, decrease, (3 dc, ch 1, 3 dc) in next ch-7 sp, skip next dc, decrease, skip next dc, work FPdc around next FPdc, ch 1, work FPdc around next FPdc, ★ (3 dc, ch 1, 3 dc) in next ch-1 sp, skip next 3 dc, work FPdc around next FPdc, ch 1, work FPdc around next FPdc; repeat from ★ around; join with slip st to top of beginning ch-3.

Rnd 9: Ch 3, (dc, ch 1, dc) in next ch-1 sp, skip next 4 dc, work FPdc around next FPdc, (2 dc, ch 1, 2 dc) in next ch-1 sp, work FPdc around next FPdc, ★ (dc, ch 1, dc) in next ch-1 sp, skip next 3 dc, work FPdc around next FPdc, (2 dc, ch 1, 2 dc) in next ch-1 sp, work FPdc around next FPdc; repeat from ★ around; join with slip st to top of beginning ch-3.

Rnd 10: Ch 4, skip next 2 dc, work FPdc around next FPdc, (3 dc, ch 1, 3 dc) in next ch-1 sp, skip next 2 dc, work FPdc around next FPdc, ★ ch 1, skip next 2 dc, work FPdc around next FPdc, (3 dc, ch 1, 3 dc) in next ch-1 sp, skip next 2 dc, work FPdc around next FPdc; repeat from ★ around; join with slip st to third ch of beginning ch-4.

Rnd 11: Ch 4, work FPdc around next FPdc, (3 dc, ch 1, 3 dc) in next ch-1 sp, skip next 3 dc, work FPdc around next FPdc, ★ ch 1, work FPdc around next FPdc, (3 dc, ch 1, 3 dc) in next ch-1 sp, skip next 3 dc, work FPdc around next FPdc; repeat from ★ around; join with slip st to third ch of beginning ch-4.

Rnd 12: Ch 3, ★ (2 dc, ch 1, 2 dc) in next ch-1 sp, work FPdc around next FPdc, (dc, ch 1, dc) in next ch-1 sp, skip next 3 dc, work FPdc around next FPdc; repeat from ★ around; join with slip st to top of beginning ch-3.

Rnd 13: Ch 3, ★ (3 dc, ch 1, 3 dc) in next ch-1 sp, skip next 2 dc, work FPdc around next FPdc, ch 1, skip next 2 dc, work FPdc around next FPdc; repeat from ★ around; join with slip st to top of beginning ch-3.

Row 14: Ch 3, ★ (3 dc, ch 1, 3 dc) in next ch-1 sp, skip next 3 dc, work FPdc around next FPdc, ch 1, work FPdc around next FPdc; repeat from ★ around; join with slip st to top of beginning ch-3.

Rnd 15: Ch 3, ★ (dc, ch 1, dc) in next ch-1 sp, skip next 3 dc, work FPdc around next FPdc, (2 dc, ch 1, 2 dc) in next ch-1 sp, work FPdc around next FPdc; repeat from ★ around; join with slip st to top of beginning ch-3.

Rnds 16-23: Repeat Rnds 10-15 once, then repeat Rnds 10 and 11 once **more**.

Finish off.

Thread tapestry needle with long end and sew base of Fsc together.

CHUNKY V'S LACE MITTS

EASY +

SHOPPING LIST

Yarn (Super Fine Weight) **SUPER FINE 1**
[1.76 ounces, 213 yards
(50 grams, 195 meters) per skein]:
☐ One skein

Crochet Hook
☐ Size E (3.5 mm)
 or size needed for gauge

Additional Supplies
☐ Tapestry needle

SIZE INFORMATION

Finished Hand Circumference:

Small - 5" (12.5 cm)
Medium - 6¼" (16 cm)
Large - 7½" (19 cm)

Size Note: We have printed the instructions for the sizes in different colors to make it easier for you to find:

- size Small in Blue
- size Medium in Pink
- size Large in Green

Instructions in Black apply to all sizes.

GAUGE INFORMATION

In Body pattern,
  2 repeats (8 sts and 8 sps) and
  6 rnds/rows = 2½" (6.25 cm)
In Cuff pattern, 10 rows = 2" (5 cm)

Gauge Swatch:

2½{3⅛-3¾}"w (flattened) x 2"h
6.25{8-9.5} cm x 5 cm

Work same as Body, page 20, through Rnd 4: 8{10-12} dc, 8{10-12} Clusters, and 8{10-12} sps.

STITCH GUIDE

🎥 FOUNDATION SINGLE CROCHET
(abbreviated Fsc)

Ch 2, insert hook under top 2 loops of second ch from hook, YO and pull up a loop *(Fig. 2b, page 30)*, YO and draw through one loop on hook (**ch made**), YO and draw through 2 loops on hook (**first Fsc made**), ★ insert hook under top 2 loops of ch at base of previous Fsc, YO and pull up a loop, YO and draw through one loop on hook (**ch made**), YO and draw through 2 loops on hook (**Fsc made**); repeat from ★ for each additional Fsc.

🎥 FRONT HALF DOUBLE CROCHET
(abbreviated front hdc)

YO, insert hook from **front** to **back** around top of next st *(Fig. 4, page 30)*, YO and pull up a loop, YO and draw through all 3 loops on hook.

🎥 BACK HALF DOUBLE CROCHET
(abbreviated back hdc)

YO, insert hook from **back** to **front** around top of next st *(Fig. 4, page 30)*, YO and pull up a loop, YO and draw through all 3 loops on hook.

🎥 CLUSTER (uses one st or sp)

★ YO, insert hook in st or sp indicated, YO and pull up a loop, YO and draw through 2 loops on hook; repeat from ★ 2 times **more**, YO and draw through all 4 loops on hook.

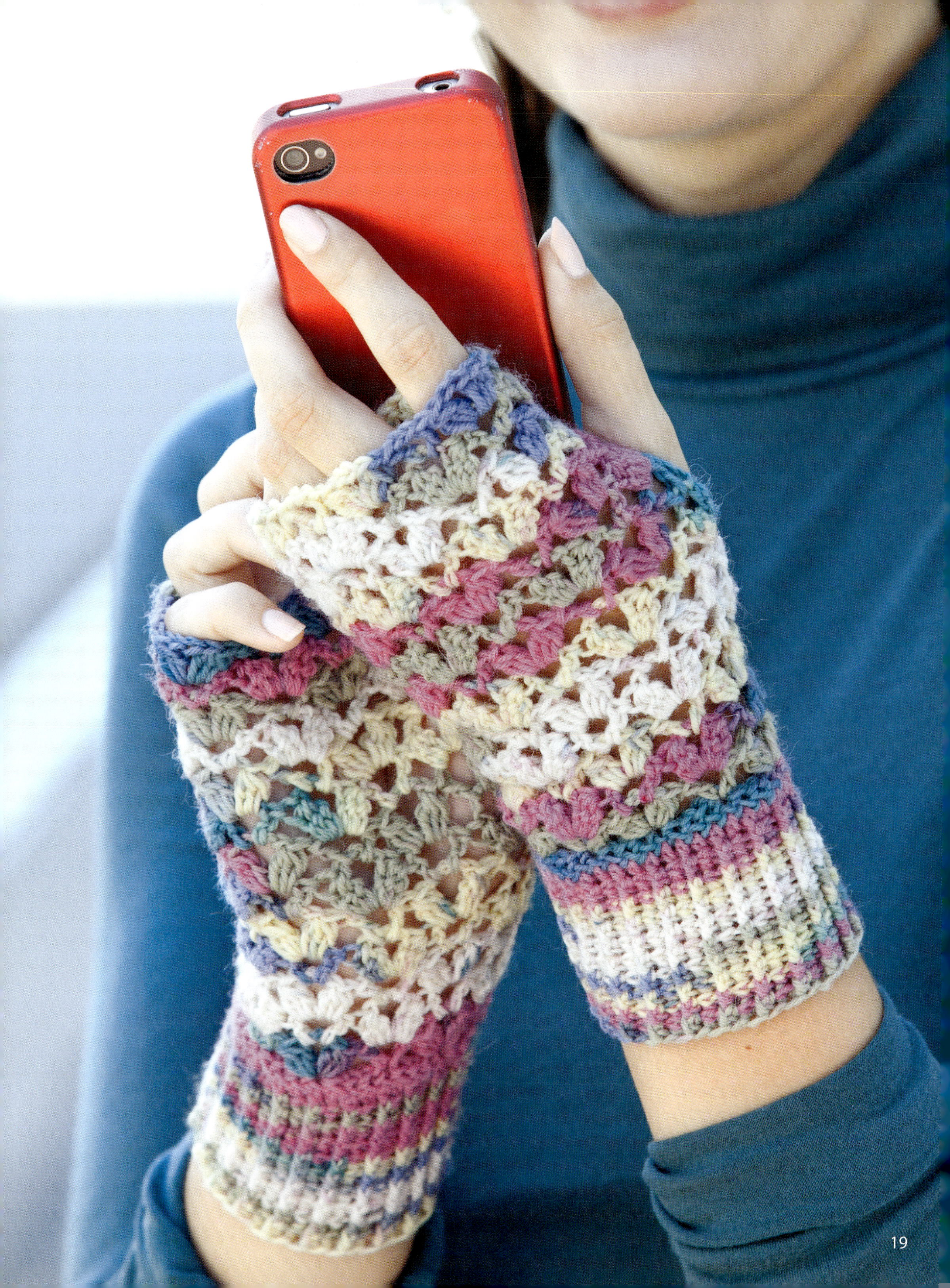

INSTRUCTIONS
Mitt (Make 2)
BODY

Foundation (Right side)**:** Work 32{40-48} Fsc; being careful **not** to twist piece, join with slip st to first Fsc to begin working in rnds.

Note: Loop a short piece of yarn around any stitch to mark Foundation as **right** side.

Rnd 1: Ch 5 (**counts as first dc plus ch 2, now and throughout**); dc in same st as joining, skip next 3 Fsc, work (Cluster, ch 3, Cluster) in next Fsc, skip next 3 Fsc, ★ (dc, ch 2, dc) in next Fsc, skip next 3 Fsc, work (Cluster, ch 3, Cluster) in next Fsc, skip next 3 Fsc; repeat from ★ around; join with slip st to first dc: 8{10-12} dc, 8{10-12} Clusters, and 8{10-12} sps.

Rnds 2 thru 4{5-5}: Turn; slip st in next Cluster and in next ch-3 sp, ch 5, dc in same sp, work (Cluster, ch 3, Cluster) in next ch-2 sp, ★ (dc, ch 2, dc) in next ch-3 sp, work (Cluster, ch 3, Cluster) in next ch-2 sp; repeat from ★ around; join with slip st to first dc.

Do **not** finish off.

THUMB OPENING

Row 1: Ch 3 (**counts as first dc, now and throughout**), turn; ★ (dc, ch 2, dc) in next ch-3 sp, work (Cluster, ch 3, Cluster) in next ch-2 sp; repeat from ★ around, dc in next dc (joining dc), do **not** join: 10{12-14} dc, 8{10-12} Clusters, and 8{10-12} sps.

Row 2: Ch 3, turn; ★ (dc, ch 2, dc) in next ch-3 sp, work (Cluster, ch 3, Cluster) in next ch-2 sp; repeat from ★ across to last 2 dc, skip next dc, dc in last dc.

Row 3: Ch 3, turn; ★ (dc, ch 2, dc) in next ch-3 sp, work (Cluster, ch 3, Cluster) in next ch-2 sp; repeat from ★ across to last 2 dc, skip next dc, dc in last dc; join with slip st to first dc to begin working in rnds.

Next Rnd: Turn; slip st in next 2 sts and in next ch-3 sp, ch 5, dc in same sp, work (Cluster, ch 3, Cluster) in next ch-2 sp, ★ (dc, ch 2, dc) in next ch-3 sp, work (Cluster, ch 3, Cluster) in next ch-2 sp; repeat from ★ around; join with slip st to first dc: 8{10-12} dc, 8{10-12} Clusters, and 8{10-12} sps.

Last 3{4-4} Rnds: Turn; slip st in next Cluster and in next ch-3 sp, ch 5, dc in same sp, work (Cluster, ch 3, Cluster) in next ch-2 sp, ★ (dc, ch 2, dc) in next ch-3 sp, work (Cluster, ch 3, Cluster) in next ch-2 sp; repeat from ★ around; join with slip st to first dc.

Finish off.

CUFF

Rnd 1: With **right** side facing and working in chs at base of Fsc, join yarn with hdc in ch at base of first Fsc *(see Joining With Hdc, page 29)*; hdc in next ch and in each ch around; join with slip st to first hdc: 32{40-48} hdc.

Rnds 2-10: Ch 2, front hdc around same st as joining, back hdc around next st, (front hdc around next st, back hdc around next st) around; skip beginning ch-2 and join with slip st to first front hdc.

Finish off.

20 www.leisurearts.com

STAGGERED CROSS STITCH MITTS

■■□□ EASY

SHOPPING LIST

Yarn (Super Fine Weight) [SUPER FINE 1]
[1.75 ounces, 166 yards
(50 grams, 152 meters) per skein]:
☐ One skein

Crochet Hook
☐ Size F (3.75 mm)
or size needed for gauge

Additional Supplies
☐ Tapestry needle

SIZE INFORMATION

Finished Hand Circumference:
Small - 6" (15 cm)
Medium - 6½" (16.5 cm)
Large - 7" (18 cm)
Size Note: We have printed the instructions for the sizes in different colors to make it easier for you to find:
• size Small in Blue
• size Medium in Pink
• size Large in Green
Instructions in Black apply to all sizes.

GAUGE INFORMATION

In Cross St pattern,
7 Cross Sts (14 dc) = 3" (7.5 cm)
and 7 rnds = 2½" (6.25 cm)

Gauge Swatch:
3{3¼-3½}"w (flattened) x 2½"h
7.5{8.25-9} cm x 6.25 cm
Work same as Cuff, page 22, through Rnd 6: 28{30-32} dc
[14{15-16} Cross Sts].

——— STITCH GUIDE ———

🎥 **FOUNDATION SINGLE CROCHET**
(abbreviated Fsc)

Ch 2, insert hook under top 2 loops of second ch from hook, YO and pull up a loop *(Fig. 2b, page 30)*, YO and draw through one loop on hook (**ch made**), YO and draw through 2 loops on hook (**first Fsc made**), ★ insert hook under top 2 loops of ch at base of previous Fsc, YO and pull up a loop, YO and draw through one loop on hook (**ch made**), YO and draw through 2 loops on hook (**Fsc made**); repeat from ★ for each additional Fsc.

🎥 **CROSS ST** (uses next 2 sts)

Skip next st, dc in next st, working **around** dc just made, dc in skipped st.

🎥 **CROSS ST INCREASE**

Dc in next st, working **around** dc just made, dc in st that previous st was worked into.

21

INSTRUCTIONS
Mitt (Make 2)
CUFF

Foundation (Right side)**:** Leaving a long end for sewing, work 28{30-32} Fsc; being careful **not** to twist piece, join with slip st to first Fsc to begin working in rnds.

Rnd 1: Ch 3 (**counts as first dc, now and throughout**), working **around** dc just made, dc in last Fsc made on Foundation (**first Cross St made**), work Cross Sts around; join with slip st to first dc: 28{30-32} dc [14{15-16} Cross Sts].

Rnds 2-9: Ch 3, working **around** dc just made, dc in last dc made on previous rnd (**first Cross St made**), work Cross Sts around; join with slip st to first dc.

BODY
THUMB GUSSET

Rnd 1: Ch 3, working **around** dc just made, dc in last dc made on previous rnd (**first Cross St made**), work 6{7-8} Cross Sts, work 2 Cross St increases, work Cross Sts across: 30{32-34} dc [15{16-17} Cross Sts].

Rnd 2: Ch 3, working **around** dc just made, dc in last dc made on previous rnd (**first Cross St made**), work 7{8-9} Cross Sts, work 2 Cross St increases, work Cross Sts across: 32{34-36} dc [16{17-18} Cross Sts].

Rnd 3: Ch 3, working **around** dc just made, dc in last dc made on previous rnd (**first Cross St made**), work 8{9-10} Cross Sts, work 2 Cross St increases, work Cross Sts across: 34{36-38} dc [17{18-19} Cross Sts].

Rnd 4: Ch 3, working **around** dc just made, dc in last dc made on previous rnd (**first Cross St made**), work 9{10-11} Cross Sts, work 2 Cross St increases, work Cross Sts across: 36{38-40} dc [18{19-20} Cross Sts].

Rnd 5: Ch 3, working **around** dc just made, dc in last dc made on previous rnd (**first Cross St made**), work 10{11-12} Cross Sts, work 2 Cross St increases, work Cross Sts across: 38{40-42} dc [19{20-21} Cross Sts].

Size Large ONLY
Rnd 6: Ch 3, working **around** dc just made, dc in last dc made on previous rnd (**first Cross St made**), work 13 Cross Sts, work 2 Cross St increases, work Cross Sts across: 44 dc [22 Cross Sts].

ALL Sizes
Next 2{2-1} Rnd(s): Ch 3, working **around** dc just made, dc in last dc made on previous rnd (**first Cross St made**), work Cross Sts around; join with slip st to first dc.

Gusset Joining Rnd: Ch 3, working **around** dc just made, dc in last dc made on previous rnd (**first Cross St made**), work 9{10-11} Cross Sts, skip next 11{11-13} dc (**thumb opening**), dc in next dc, working **around** dc just made, dc in first skipped dc (**Cross St made**), work Cross Sts around; join with slip st to first dc: 28{30-32} dc [14{15-16} Cross Sts].

Last 5 Rnds: Ch 3, working **around** dc just made, dc in last dc made on previous rnd (**first Cross St made**), work Cross Sts around; join with slip st to first dc.

Finish off.

Thread tapestry needle with long end and sew base of Fsc together.

23

TWISTED CABLE COLUMNS MITTS

▬▬▬▬ **INTERMEDIATE**

SHOPPING LIST

Yarn (Super Fine Weight) **SUPER FINE 1**
[3.5 ounces, 438 yards
(100 grams, 400 meters) per skein]:
☐ One skein

Crochet Hook
☐ Size F (3.75 mm)
or size needed for gauge

Additional Supplies
☐ Tapestry needle

SIZE INFORMATION

Finished Hand Circumference:

Small - 6¼" (16 cm)
Medium - 6¾" (17 cm)
Large - 7¼" (18.5 cm)

Size Note: We have printed the instructions for the sizes in different colors to make it easier for you to find:
• size Small in Blue
• size Medium in Pink
• size Large in Green

Instructions in Black apply to all sizes.

In Body pattern,
2 repeats (14 sts) = 2¼" (5.75 cm)
and 8 rnds = 1⅞" (4.75 cm)

GAUGE INFORMATION

Gauge Swatch:
3⅛{3⅜-3⅝}"w (flattened) x 2"h
8{8.5-9.25} cm x 5 cm
Work same as Body, page 26, through Rnd 8: 34{36-39} sts and 5{6-6} chs.

STITCH GUIDE

🎥 FOUNDATION SINGLE CROCHET (abbreviated Fsc)

Ch 2, insert hook under top 2 loops of second ch from hook, YO and pull up a loop *(Fig. 2b, page 30)*, YO and draw through one loop on hook (**ch made**), YO and draw through 2 loops on hook (**first Fsc made**), ★ insert hook under top 2 loops of ch at base of previous Fsc, YO and pull up a loop, YO and draw through one loop on hook (**ch made**), YO and draw through 2 loops on hook (**Fsc made**); repeat from ★ for each additional Fsc.

🎥 FRONT POST DOUBLE CROCHET (abbreviated FPdc)

YO, insert hook from **front** to **back** around post of st indicated *(Fig. 3, page 30)*, YO and pull up a loop (3 loops on hook), (YO and draw through 2 loops on hook) twice.

🎥 CROSS ST (uses next 3 Fsc)

Skip next 2 Fsc, dc in next Fsc, ch 1, working **around** dc just made, dc in first skipped Fsc.

🎥 FRONT POST CROSS ST (abbreviated FP Cross St) (uses next 3 sts)

Skip next 2 sts, work FPdc around next st, ch 1, working in **front** of last FPdc made, work FPdc around first skipped st.

🎥 FRONT HALF DOUBLE CROCHET (abbreviated front hdc)

YO, insert hook from **front** to **back** around top of next st *(Fig. 4, page 30)*, YO and pull up a loop, YO and draw through all 3 loops on hook.

🎥 BACK HALF DOUBLE CROCHET (abbreviated back hdc)

YO, insert hook from **back** to **front** around top of next st *(Fig. 4, page 30)*, YO and pull up a loop, YO and draw through all 3 loops on hook.

🎥 DOUBLE CROCHET 2 TOGETHER (abbreviated dc2tog) (uses next 2 sts)

★ YO, insert hook in **next** st, YO and pull up a loop, YO and draw through 2 loops on hook; repeat from ★ once **more**, YO and draw through all 3 loops on hook (**counts as one dc**).

24   www.leisurearts.com

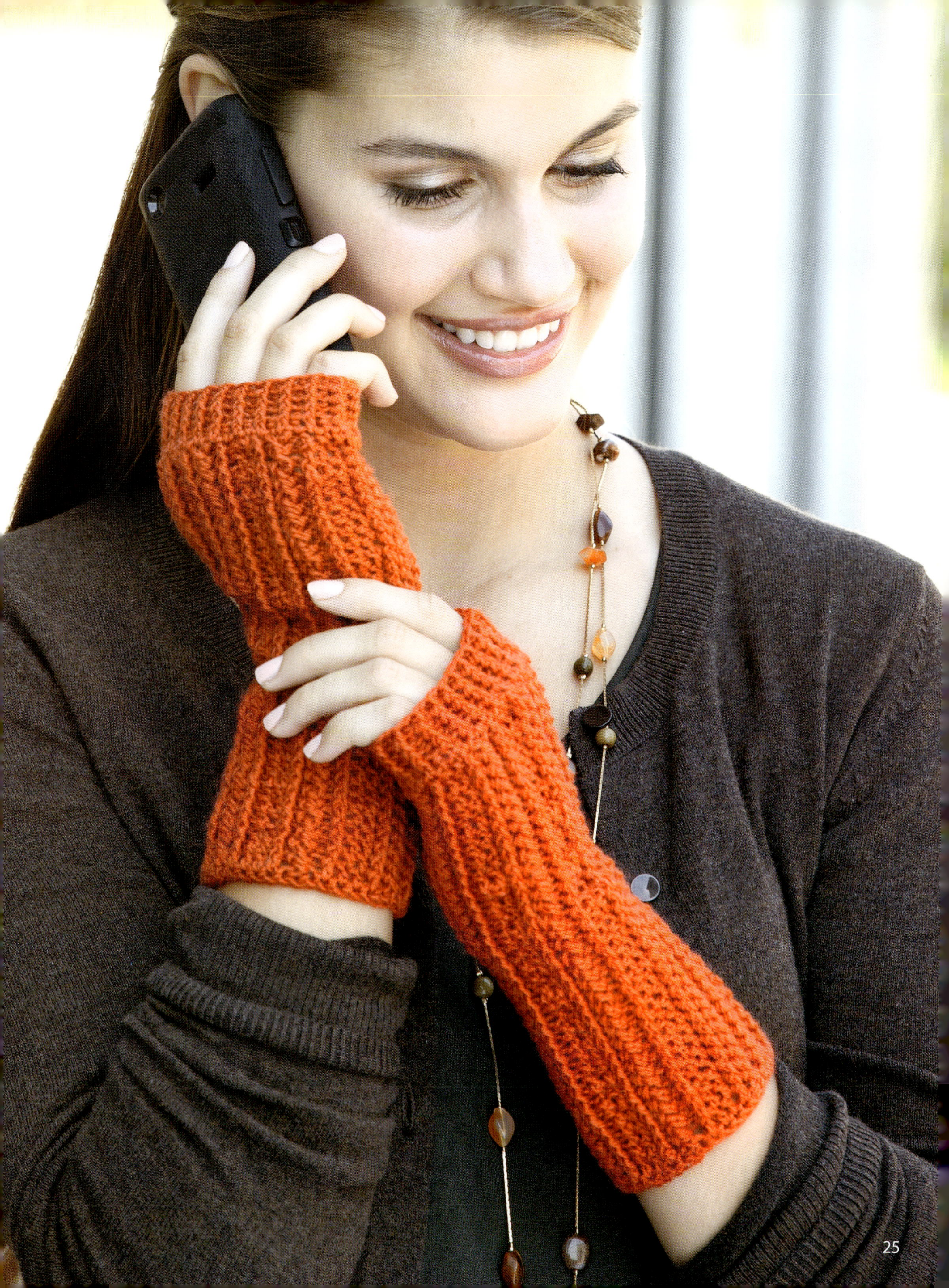

INSTRUCTIONS
Mitt (Make 2)
BODY

Foundation (Right side): Leaving a long end for sewing, work 39{42-45} Fsc; being careful **not** to twist piece, join with slip st to first Fsc to begin working in rnds.

Rnd 1: Ch 3 (**counts as first dc, now and throughout**), dc in next 3{1-3} Fsc, work Cross St, (dc in next 4 Fsc, work Cross St) around to last 4{2-3} sts, dc in last 4{2-3} sts; join with slip st to first dc: 34{36-39} sts and 5{6-6} chs.

Rnds 2-22: Ch 3, dc in next 2{0-2} dc *(see Zeros, page 29)*, work FPdc around next st, work FP Cross St, work FPdc around next st, ★ dc in next 2 dc, work FPdc around next st, work FP Cross St, work FPdc around next st; repeat from ★ around to last 3{1-2} st(s), dc in last 3{1-2} st(s); join with slip st to first dc.

Do **not** finish off.

THUMB OPENING
Right-Hand Mitt

Rnd 23: Ch 3, dc in next 2{0-2} dc, work FPdc around next FPdc, ★ work FP Cross St, work FPdc around next FPdc, dc in next 2 dc, work FPdc around next FPdc; repeat from ★ 2{3-3} times **more**, dc in next st, 2 dc in next ch-1 sp, dc in next st, work FPdc around next FPdc, dc in next 2 dc, work FPdc around next FPdc, work FP Cross St, work FPdc around next FPdc, dc in last 3{1-2} st(s); join with slip st to first dc: 36{38-41} sts and 4{5-5} chs.

Rnd 24: Ch 3, dc in next 2{0-2} dc, work FPdc around next FPdc, ★ work FP Cross St, work FPdc around next FPdc, dc in next 2 dc, work FPdc around next FPdc; repeat from ★ 2{3-3} times **more**, dc in next dc, ch 8, skip next 2 dc (**thumb opening**), dc in next dc, work FPdc around next FPdc, dc in next 2 dc, work FPdc around next FPdc, work FP Cross St, work FPdc around next FPdc, dc in last 3{1-2} st(s); join with slip st to first dc: 34{36-39} sts, one ch-8 sp, and 4{5-5} chs.

Rnd 25: Ch 3, dc in next 2{0-2} dc, work FPdc around next FPdc, ★ work FP Cross St, work FPdc around next FPdc, dc in next 2 dc, work FPdc around next FPdc; repeat from ★ 2{3-3} times **more**, dc in next dc, sc in third ch of ch-8, 2 sc in ch-8 sp, sc in sixth ch of ch-8, dc in next dc, work FPdc around next FPdc, dc in next 2 dc, work FPdc around next FPdc, work FP Cross St, work FPdc around next FPdc, dc in last 3{1-2} st(s); join with slip st to first dc: 38{40-43} sts and 4{5-5} chs.

Rnd 26: Ch 3, dc in next 2{0-2} dc, work FPdc around next FPdc, ★ work FP Cross St, work FPdc around next FPdc, dc in next 2 dc, work FPdc around next FPdc; repeat from ★ 2{3-3} times **more**, dc2tog 3 times, work FPdc around next FPdc, dc in next 2 dc, work FPdc around next FPdc, work FP Cross St, work FPdc around next FPdc, dc in last 3{1-2} st(s); join with slip st to first dc: 35{37-40} sts and 4{5-5} chs.

Left-Hand Mitt
Rnd 23: Ch 3, dc in next 2{0-2} dc, work FPdc around next FPdc, work FP Cross St, work FPdc around next FPdc, dc in next 2 dc, work FPdc around next FPdc, dc in next st, 2 dc in next ch-1 sp, dc in next st, work FPdc around next FPdc, ★ dc in next 2 dc, work FPdc around next FPdc, work FP Cross St, work FPdc around

next FPdc; repeat from ★ 2{3-3} times **more**; dc in last 3{1-2} st(s); join with slip st to first dc: 36{38-41} sts and 4{5-5} chs.

Rnd 24: Ch 3, dc in next 2{0-2} dc, work FPdc around next FPdc, work FP Cross St, work FPdc around next FPdc, dc in next 2 dc, work FPdc around next FPdc, dc in next dc, ch 8, skip next 2 dc (**thumb opening**), dc in next dc, work FPdc around next FPdc, ★ dc in next 2 dc, work FPdc around next FPdc, work FP Cross St, work FPdc around next FPdc; repeat from ★ 2{3-3} times **more**, dc in last 3{1-2} st(s); join with slip st to first dc: 34{36-39} sts, one ch-8 sp, and 4{5-5} chs.

Rnd 25: Ch 3, dc in next 2{0-2} dc, work FPdc around next FPdc, work FP Cross St, work FPdc around next FPdc, dc in next 2 dc, work FPdc around next FPdc, dc in next dc, sc in third ch of ch-8, 2 sc in ch-8 sp, sc in sixth ch of ch-8, dc in next dc, work FPdc around next FPdc, ★ dc in next 2 dc, work FPdc around next FPdc, work FP Cross St, work FPdc around next FPdc; repeat from ★ 2{3-3} times **more**, dc in last 3{1-2} st(s); join with slip st to first dc: 38{40-43} sts and 4{5-5} chs.

Rnd 26: Ch 3, dc in next 2{0-2} dc, work FPdc around next FPdc, work FP Cross St, work FPdc around next FPdc, dc in next 2 dc, work FPdc

around next FPdc, dc2tog 3 times, work FPdc around next FPdc, ★ dc in next 2 dc, work FPdc around next FPdc, work FP Cross St, work FPdc around next FPdc; repeat from ★ 2{3-3} times **more**, dc in last 3{1-2} st(s); join with slip st to first dc: 35{37-40} sts and 4{5-5} chs.

Both Mitts
Rnds 27-32: Ch 3, dc in next 2{0-2} dc, work FPdc around next st, work FP Cross St, work FPdc around next st, ★ dc in next 2 dc, work FPdc around next st, work FP Cross St, work FPdc around next st; repeat from ★ around to last 3{1-2} st(s), dc in last 3{1-2} st(s); join with slip st to first dc.

Do **not** finish off.

FINGER RIBBING
Rnd 1: Ch 2, hdc in same st as joining 0{1-0} time(s), hdc in next st and in each st and ch-1 sp around; skip beginning ch-2 and join with slip st to first hdc: 38{42-44} hdc.

Rnds 2-5: Ch 2, front hdc around same st as joining, back hdc around next st, (front hdc around next hdc, back hdc around next hdc) around; skip beginning ch-2 and join with slip st to first front hdc.

Finish off.

Thread tapestry needle with long end and sew base of Fsc together.

27

GENERAL INSTRUCTIONS

ABBREVIATIONS

ch(s)	chain(s)
cm	centimeters
dc	double crochet(s)
dc2tog	double crochet 2 together
Fsc	Foundation single crochet(s)
FP	Front Post
FPdc	Front Post double crochet(s)
FPtr	Front Post treble crochet(s)
hdc	half double crochet(s)
mm	millimeters
sc	single crochet(s)
sp(s)	space(s)
st(s)	stitch(es)
tr	treble crochet(s)
YO	yarn over

SYMBOLS & TERMS

★ — work instructions following ★ as many **more** times as indicated in addition to the first time.

( ) or [ ] — work enclosed instructions **as many** times as specified by the number immediately following **or** work enclosed instructions in stitch or space indicated **or** contains explanatory remarks.

colon (:) — the numbers given after a colon at the end of a row or round denote the number of stitches or spaces you should have on that row or round.

BEGINNER		Projects for first-time crocheters using basic stitches. Minimal shaping.
EASY		Projects using yarn with basic stitches, repetitive stitch patterns, simple color changes, and simple shaping and finishing.
INTERMEDIATE		Projects using a variety of techniques, such as basic lace patterns or color patterns, mid-level shaping and finishing.
EXPERIENCED		Projects with intricate stitch patterns, techniques and dimension, such as non-repeating patterns, multi-color techniques, fine threads, small hooks, detailed shaping and refined finishing.

CROCHET TERMINOLOGY

UNITED STATES		INTERNATIONAL
slip stitch (slip st)	=	single crochet (sc)
single crochet (sc)	=	double crochet (dc)
half double crochet (hdc)	=	half treble crochet (htr)
double crochet (dc)	=	treble crochet (tr)
treble crochet (tr)	=	double treble crochet (dtr)
double treble crochet (dtr)	=	triple treble crochet (ttr)
triple treble crochet (tr tr)	=	quadruple treble crochet (qtr)
skip	=	miss

Yarn Weight Symbol & Names	LACE 0	SUPER FINE 1	FINE 2	LIGHT 3	MEDIUM 4	BULKY 5	SUPER BULKY 6
Type of Yarns in Category	Fingering, 10-count crochet thread	Sock, Fingering Baby	Sport, Baby	DK, Light Worsted	Worsted, Afghan, Aran	Chunky, Craft, Rug	Bulky, Roving
Crochet Gauge* Ranges in Single Crochet to 4" (10 cm)	32-42 double crochets**	21-32 sts	16-20 sts	12-17 sts	11-14 sts	8-11 sts	5-9 sts
Advised Hook Size Range	Steel*** 6,7,8 Regular hook B-1	B-1 to E-4	E-4 to 7	7 to I-9	I-9 to K-10.5	K-10.5 to M-13	M-13 and larger

*GUIDELINES ONLY: The chart above reflects the most commonly used gauges and hook sizes for specific yarn categories.

** Lace weight yarns are usually crocheted on larger-size hooks to create lacy openwork patterns. Accordingly, a gauge range is difficult to determine. Always follow the gauge stated in your pattern.

*** Steel crochet hooks are sized differently from regular hooks--the higher the number the smaller the hook, which is the reverse of regular hook sizing.

CROCHET HOOKS

U.S.	B-1	C-2	D-3	E-4	F-5	G-6	H-8	I-9	J-10	K-10½	L-11	M/N-13	N/P-15	P/Q	Q	S
Metric - mm	2.25	2.75	3.25	3.5	3.75	4	5	5.5	6	6.5	8	9	10	15	16	19

www.leisurearts.com

GAUGE

Exact gauge is **essential** for proper size. Before beginning you Mitts, make the sample swatch given in the individual instructions in the yarn and hook specified. After completing the swatch, measure it, counting your stitches and rows/rounds carefully. If your swatch is larger or smaller than specified, **make another, changing hook size to get the correct gauge**. Keep trying until you find the size hook that will give you the specified gauge.

SIZING

Measure around the widest part of your hand, usually across the knuckles *(Fig. 1)*. Mitt sizing is based on this measurement, so pick a finished measurement approximately ½" to 1" (1.25 cm to 2.5 cm) smaller than your hand measurement to obtain a comfortable fit.

Fig. 1

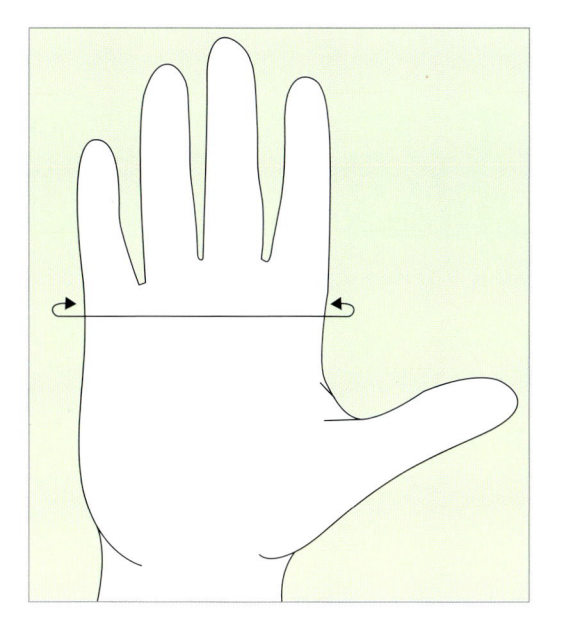

ZEROS

To consolidate the length of an involved pattern, Zeros are sometimes used so that all sizes can be combined. For example, dc in next 2{0-2} dc means the small and the large sizes would dc in the next 2 dc, and the medium size would do nothing.

JOINING WITH SC

When instructed to join with sc, begin with a slip knot on hook. Insert hook in stitch or space indicated, YO and pull up a loop, YO and draw through both loops on hook.

JOINING WITH HDC

When instructed to join with hdc, begin with a slip knot on hook. YO, holding loop on hook, insert hook in stitch or space indicated, YO and pull up a loop, YO and draw through all 3 loops on hook.

WORKING INTO THE CHAIN

Method 1: When instructed to work in back ridge of chains, work only in loops indicated by arrows *(Fig. 2a)*.
Method 2: Insert hook under top 2 loops of each ch *(Fig. 2b)*.

Fig. 2a

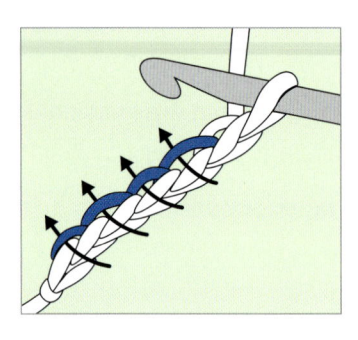

Fig. 2b

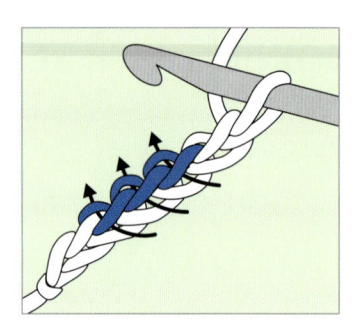

POST STITCH

Work around post of stitch indicated, inserting hook in direction of arrow *(Fig. 3)*.

Fig. 3

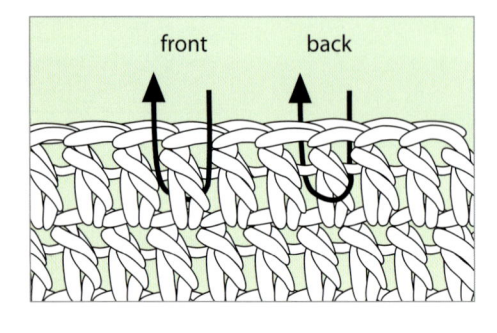

WORKING AROUND TOP OF A STITCH

Work around top of stitch indicated, inserting hook in direction of arrow *(Fig. 4)*.

Fig. 4

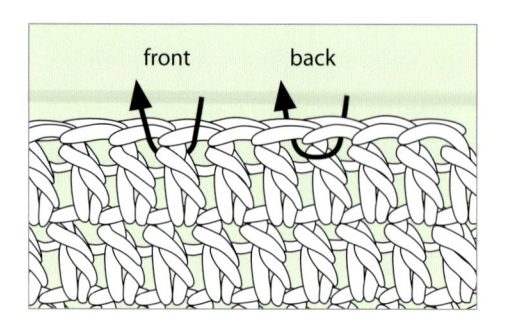

WORKING IN A SPACE BEFORE A STITCH

When instructed to work in a space **before** a stitch or in spaces **between** stitches, insert hook in space indicated by arrow *(Fig. 5)*.

Fig. 5

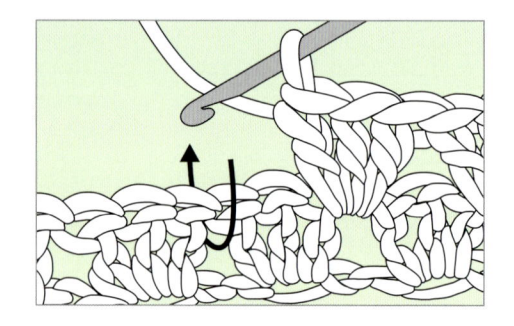

YARN INFORMATION

The Mitts in this leaflet were made using Super Fine Weight yarn. Any brand of Super Fine Weight yarn may be used. It is best to refer to the yardage/meters when determining how many balls or skeins to purchase. Remember, to achieve the same look, it is the weight of yarn that is important, not the brand of yarn.

For your convenience, listed below are the specific yarns used to create our photography models.

SIMPLE BEGINNER LACE MITTS
Red Heart® Heart & Sole®
#3970 Faded Jeans

CABLED SHELLS MITTS
Red Heart® Stardust™
#1701 Pink

SMALL V-STITCH WRISTERS
Loops & Threads™ Luxury Sock™
#1 Spring Fling

CHUNKY V'S LACE MITTS
Red Heart® Heart & Sole®
#3950 Watercolor Stripe

DIAMOND BACK MITTS
Lion Brand® Sock-Ease™
#138 Grape Soda

STAGGERED CROSS STITCH MITTS
Patons® Kroy Socks™
#55017 Brown Rose Marl

SEASHELL MITTS
Patons® Kroy Socks™
#55129 Aqua Fleck

TWISTED CABLE COLUMNS MITTS
Lion Brand® Sock-Ease™
#133 Circus Peanut

MEET THE DESIGNER

ANDEE GRAVES, the owner of Two Hands Healing and Creative Arts, teaches crochet and writes about crochet techniques, designing, and healthy crafting practices for her blog, http://mamas2hands.wordpress.com, as well as other online publications.

Her design work is grounded in years of experimenting with crochet techniques and stitch patterns. She combines this with an understanding of fabrics and garment construction gleaned from her extensive sewing experience.

She retired in 2010 after 10-plus years as a licensed massage therapist. She now devotes more time to her designing and writing activities, which includes her work as a freelance health and wellness writer.

Andee finds crochet to be an exciting fiberart for exploring both sculptural and wearable designs. She says, "I am endlessly intrigued by the 'magic' of creating fabric or an object from nothing but hook and string."

Andee lives in the mountains of Colorado with her husband and two sons.

We have made every effort to ensure that these instructions are accurate and complete. We cannot, however, be responsible for human error, typographical mistakes, or variations in individual work.

Production Team: Technical Writer/Editor - Linda A. Daley; Editorial Writer - Susan McManus Johnson; Senior Graphic Artist - Lora Puls; Graphic Artist - Becca Snider Tally; Photo Stylist - Angela Alexander; and Photographer - Jason Masters.

Copyright © 2013 by Leisure Arts, Inc., 5701 Ranch Drive, Little Rock, AR 72223, www.leisurearts.com. All rights reserved. This publication is protected under federal copyright laws. Reprodction or distribution of this publication or any other Leisure Arts publication, including publications which are out of print, is prohibited unless specifically authorized. This includes, but is not limited to, any form of reproduction or distribution on or through the Internet, including posting, scanning or e-mail transmission.

Your opinion matters!

WE WOULD LOVE TO HEAR if our online video instructions and the new format of our publications are helpful to you!

PLEASE SHARE your comments and suggestions at www.facebook.com/Official.LeisureArts